Put Beginning Readers on the Right Track with
ALL ABOARD READING™

The All Aboard Reading series is especially for beginning readers. Written by noted authors and illustrated in full color, these are books that children really and truly *want* to read—books to excite their imagination, tickle their funny bone, expand their interests, and support their feelings. With three different reading levels, All Aboard Reading lets you choose which books are most appropriate for your children and their growing abilities.

Level 1—for Preschool through First Grade Children
Level 1 books have very few lines per page, very large type, easy words, lots of repetition, and pictures with visual "cues" to help children figure out the words on the page.

Level 2—for First Grade to Third Grade Children
Level 2 books are printed in slightly smaller type than Level 1 books. The stories are more complex, but there is still lots of repetition in the text and many pictures. The sentences are quite simple and are broken up into short lines to make reading easier.

Level 3—for Second Grade through Third Grade Children
Level 3 books have considerably longer texts, use harder words and more complicated sentences.

All Aboard for happy reading!

To Rosie —J.M.

This book is dedicated to
Joy and George Adamson,
who truly believed that
all animals are "born free" —S.D.

Special thanks to James G. Doherty, General Curator, Bronx Zoo,
Wildlife Conservation Park.

Text copyright © 1994 by Joyce Milton. Illustrations copyright © 1994 by Silvia Duran. All
rights reserved. Published by Grosset & Dunlap, Inc., a member of The Putnam & Grosset
Group, New York. ALL ABOARD READING is a trademark of The Putnam & Grosset Group.
GROSSET & DUNLAP is a trademark of Grosset & Dunlap, Inc. Published simultaneously in
Canada. Printed in the U.S.A.

Library of Congress Cataloging-in-Publication Data

Milton, Joyce.
   Big cats / by Joyce Milton ; illustrated by Silvia Duran.
     p.   cm. — (All aboard reading)
   "Level 2, grades 1-3."
    1. Felidae—Juvenile literature.   2. Cats—Juvenile literature. [1. Felidae. 2. Cats.]
  I. Duran, Silvia, ill. II. Title. III. Series.
  QL737.C23M555 1994
  599.74'428—dc20
                                                  94-7361
                                                  CIP
ISBN 0-448-40564-4 (pbk.) A B C D E F G H I J   AC
ISBN 0-448-40565-2 (GB) A B C D E F G H I J

ALL
ABOARD
READING™

Level 2
Grades 1-3

BIG CATS

By Joyce Milton
Illustrated by Silvia Duran

Grosset & Dunlap • New York

In Africa the noontime sun is very hot.

A thorn tree is a cool place

for a leopard to take a nap.

But she does not sleep for long.

The leopard is hungry.

She sees a herd of zebras.

The zebras don't know the leopard is near.

The leopard's spots make her hard to see.

Now, quietly, the leopard moves
through the tall grass.

The zebras sniff the air.

Danger is near!

They all run.

For one very young zebra, it is too late.

The leopard drags the zebra

up into the tree.

She will eat it there.

The leopard is a meat-eater.

She must hunt to stay alive.

Like all cats,

leopards are built for hunting.

They have sharp teeth.

And long, hooked claws.

The leopard pushes her claws out

when she attacks.

Then she pulls them back in.

claws out

claws in

Cats can run fast,

but they get tired quickly.

Most of the time they sneak up on animals.

Then they pounce!

At night it is easier for cats

to get close to animals

without scaring them away.

So the leopard often sleeps by day
and goes hunting after sundown.
Cats can see in the dark
much better than people can.

Leopards are big cats.

Tigers are big cats, too.

So are lions and jaguars

and cougars and cheetahs.

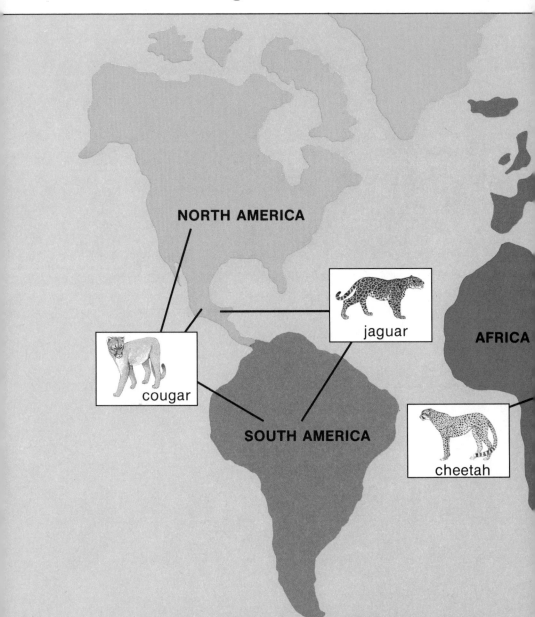

A pet cat usually weighs 10 or 12 pounds.

Big cats can weigh hundreds of pounds.

This map of the world

shows where big cats live.

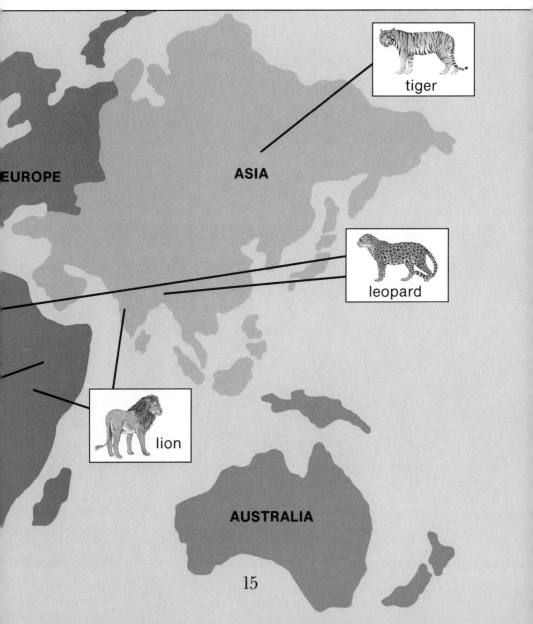

tiger

EUROPE

ASIA

leopard

lion

AUSTRALIA

15

The biggest big cat in the world
is the tiger.
A male tiger can weigh
up to 600 pounds.

Some tigers can be 7 feet long.

That's not counting the tail!

Most tigers live in the forest.

Each tiger has its own hunting ground.

Tigers are very good at hiding.

You might never know one is near.

How can you tell if you are

in a tiger's hunting ground?

You can look for claw marks on trees.

A tiger's claw marks

warn other tigers to keep away.

There are many strange and scary
stories about tigers.
Some say that a man or a woman
can turn into a weretiger.
Like a werewolf, a weretiger
roams the forest at night.
It looks for humans to eat.
Weretigers are not real.
But a few tigers do become man-eaters.
Usually the tigers are too old and sick
to catch wild animals anymore.
Almost all healthy tigers
try to stay away from people.

Most big cats are loners.

They live alone.

They hunt alone.

But lions enjoy company.

They often live and hunt in groups

called prides.

The male lion has a thick, shaggy mane.

That big mane makes it easy

for other animals

to see the male—

and stay out of his way!

Female lions do most of the hunting.

The male lion guards

the pride and their home.

He will fight strange lions.

But he would rather scare them off

with a loud roar.

The lion's roar says:

"HERE I AM! THIS IS MY HOME!"

Lions spend most of the day

taking it easy.

The grown-up lions take catnaps.

The cubs pretend to fight each other.

But the lion's life isn't always easy.

For part of the year, the plains are dry.

There isn't enough water to drink.

Or animals to hunt.

Many cubs starve.

A lion has to be strong and lucky

to stay alive.

Most cats don't like to go into the water.

But jaguars do.

They are very good swimmers.

A jaguar will even go fishing.

The big cat stands in the river.

A fish swims by him.

SMACK!

The jaguar hits it hard with his paw.

Fish for dinner!

Jaguars look a lot
like leopards.
But their spots
are different.

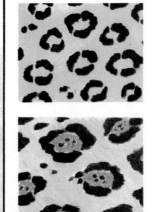

leopard

jaguar

There are no lions or tigers in America.

But there are cougars.

The cougar is the biggest cat found here.

Cougars live in the mountains.

They are great jumpers.

Cougar kittens practice jumping

from rock to rock.

The cougar has other names, too—

mountain lion...puma...or panther.

The cat that is called

the black panther

is really a leopard.

Every now and then,
some leopards give birth
to black cubs.

Up close you can see
that a black leopard's fur
is spotted.
The spots are different
shades of black.

The cheetah is another spotted cat.

But it looks different

from the leopard and the jaguar.

It is thinner.

Its legs are longer.

Of all the animals in the world,

the cheetah is the fastest.

It can run 60 miles an hour—

as fast as a car.

Hundreds of years ago,

kings in India kept tame cheetahs

and used them for hunting.

All cats—

from jungle tigers

to pets—

are alike in lots of ways.

Their tongues are rough,
like sandpaper.
They have sharp teeth
and claws.

Pet cats do lots of things that big cats do.

They sharpen their claws by scratching.

They love to hunt.

Sometimes a kitten will pretend

that an old sock is alive,

just for the fun of pouncing on it.

Like big cats,
pet cats spend lots of time
licking themselves clean.

They like to stretch—
just like big cats.

And they love to take catnaps, too.

When a pet cat is happy

it will purr and purr.

Do lions and tigers purr?

Yes, they do.

Pet cats eat food
from the grocery store.
This is one big difference
between them and big cats.

People take care of pet cats.
Big cats have always been able
to take care of themselves.
But today, that is changing.

Lions, tigers, and other big cats

need wide plains and thick jungles.

But people need land, too.

So there is less room for wild animals.

Some countries have set aside
huge parks for wild animals.

Visitors from around the world
come to see the big cats.

Will there be any big cats living free

one hundred years from now?

Yes.

But only if we care about

saving the big cats' homes.